BODY LANGUAGE

poems by

JANINE DEBAISE

MAIN STREET RAG PUBLISHING COMPANY
CHARLOTTE, NORTH CAROLINA

Library of Congress Control Number: 2019951694

ISBN: 978-1-59948-775-5

Produced in the United States of America

Main Street Rag
PO Box 690100
Charlotte, NC 28227
www.MainStreetRag.com

Acknowledgments

The author thanks the journals in which these poems originally appeared.

Baltimore Review: "Caged"
Bitter Oleander: "Giverny at Dusk," "The Waters of Round Lake"
California Quarterly: "Paris Flower Shop"
The Chariton Review: "Notre Dame"
Comstock Review: "Bird Market"
Fireweed: "Sacred Tears"
Frontiers: A Journal for Women Studies: "Chrysalis," "Sex Education"
Fourth River: Nature and Culture: "Woven"
Kalliope: "Shopping in Montmartre"
Louisville Review: "La Vedette du Pont Neuf"
The Main Street Rag: "Shining Wet"
Mad Poets Review: "Sometimes Attracts, Sometimes Repels"
Manzanita Quarterly Literary Review: "Doing Chi Gung with Judy"
Midwifery Today: "Birth Plan"
Minnesota Review: "What we Learn"
North American Review: "Evening Visit"
Owen Wister Review: "I'm Just Here to do the Flowers"
River Oak Review: "Still Life in Pine Woods"
Roanoke Review: "Afternoon Reiki"
Seattle Review: "Tobey House"
Syracuse Cultural Workers Women Artists Datebook: "Beauty Ritual,"
     "Dress Up"
13th Moon: "Ancient Rhythm"
Unwound: "Laptop"

for Shannon
my wonderful, smart, beautiful daughter

and for women friends
who share their stories

may you remain forever wild

Contents

Other voices

This is my body

What we learn

EVERY GIRL'S DREAM

I just found out something
that has changed my life,
given me hope.

My breasts are the same size as Barbie's.

Yes, it's true. I could be the woman
of the American dream. It's within my grasp.

Okay, I know what you're thinking.
And you're right. I need to lose
sixteen inches from my waist.
And eight inches from my hips.
But I think that's possible.

I'm going to start now
to grow my hair long.
Dye it blond. Brush it
with polyurethane to make it stiff.

My name isn't Barbie.
But that's okay. The first Barbie doll
was named Lilli. She was sold in porn shops
in Switzerland as a gag gift for men.

Of course, I'll have to learn how to walk around on my toes.
No more hiking boots or comfy sneakers.
It's high heels from now on.

But it will be worth it.
Every second, somewhere in the world,
two Barbie dolls are sold. Sixty-four
have been sold since I began this poem.
Everyone knows: she's the perfect woman.
And I am going to look just like her.

My legs need to be three feet longer.
And of course, I'll have to keep breastfeeding forever
so that my breasts don't get smaller.
But I can do that.

Maybe you think it's strange for a sex object
to breastfeed a baby. Madonna and I—
we've changed that image.

I would need some minor surgery. My neck is way too short.
I'm thinking of getting a transplant from a swan.
Yeah, I know how people in Manlius got all upset
when teenagers killed a swan for no good reason.
But this would be a good reason.

I could be Barbie.

When women get in touch with the child inside
they find that child holding a doll
and she's Barbie.

I could be the object of hope for every American woman.

And I'd win the prize.
Barbie's reward.
Her one goal, her one dream.

To be with Ken.
A man with a year-round tan
a perpetual smile
and no penis at all.

What more could a woman want?

I'M JUST HERE TO DO THE FLOWERS

It has been suggested.
I mean, there's this shortage of priests.
(Between you and me, I think
it's the celibacy thing.)

An open mike at Sunday Mass.
But I'm not so sure it's a good idea.

I mean, what if ...
a woman gets up to speak?
What if a woman gets up to speak
and she's not wearing a bra?

There'd have to be all sorts of rules.
No woman who's nursing a baby—what if
milk leaked through her blouse
in front of the congregation?

And no woman with PMS. Think of the sermon
we'd get. She'd wake up the dead.

No woman going through the change.
No woman who wants the church to change.

What if an attractive woman takes the mike?
And the young fellows start watching
the way her chest moves when she talks?
What if the priest starts watching her?

(Between you and me, it's that
whole celibacy thing.)

How would we regulate what they say?
I've heard that some women have the nerve
to stand up in front of a microphone
and use the word breast.

My mother only used that word
when she was serving
chicken. And most of the time
we just called it white meat.

I've been up on this altar before. Every week.
I go in early Saturday to do the flowers.
I snip off dead buds, put in fresh water.

We've had a woman here all along. The blessed mother.
If statues could talk—we could give the mike to her.
This woman once held the Son of God
in her arms, breastfed him, changed his diaper.

If I were a sculptor, I wouldn't make her
so young, so perfect. I would chisel in some wrinkles.
And stretch marks. A grey hair or two.
I wouldn't hide the glory.

It's not for me to say, of course.

I have no voice
in this church.

Only a body.

DRESS UP

The paper doll doesn't have breasts or belly

The glamorous evening
gowns fit tight
around the ankles
with little tabs that keep
the legs together

You can put her in a cardboard stand

But mostly she lies
on her back
staring at the ceiling
with that painted-on smile

SLICING MEAT

The magician cut me
into three pieces

head
torso
feet

and the audience
applauded

SOMETIMES ATTRACTS, SOMETIMES REPELS

He told me that his penis was magnetic.
This explained a lot.

The words on my refrigerator kept shifting
toward him while he talked.

I remember the time he got stuck
to the back of his old pickup.

He stood there for hours,
beer in hand, awkwardly shifting.

When I was with him,
I had trouble finding true north.

My sister has steel pins in her elbow.
I worry what would happen if she got near him.

He finds women who are lost,
who turn to him for help.

Look, he says, look.
The compass points to my cock.

A WOMAN'S BODY

Tourists in Washington stare at a Peruvian mummy
preserved for 500 years by a mountain glacier.

A frozen thirteen-year-old girl
discovered in the Andes.

Reporters in Gouverneur crowd the courthouse
to snap pictures of the woman

who insists on prosecuting
the five men who raped her.

Carrier Corporation came to the rescue.
They built a refrigerated case

to preserve the frozen girl.
So the public can stare at her. Forever.

The woman in the bar in Gouverneur was drunk,
passed out on the floor in the ladies' room

so the men carried her unconscious body into a booth
and one at a time, the five men raped her.

They named her Juanita after the
man who found her body. No one knows

what name her mother gave her
when she first pulled her wet and squirming

from her own body. Or what name she used when
she played with other children in the village.

Krista's name is in the headlines,
her picture on the front page.

Reporters say they cannot protect
a victim of rape if she decides to seek justice.

Archeologists say the Incan girl was fed a ritual meal
laced with heavy narcotics.

She knelt on the ground and a man
with a club fractured her skull.

They wrapped her body in a cocoon of cloth,
put corn and cocoa leaves in the tomb.

The five men from Gouverneur pled guilty.
How could they not? They had bragged the story

all over that north country town.
"It's not like she was a virgin," people said.

Time Magazine says the ice maiden is a great discovery
for science. An important object of study.

She was a thirteen-year-old virgin
offered by the Incas to the Volcano Ampato.

We don't call it murder
because it was part of their culture.

The judge fined the five men.
Seven hundred and fifty dollars.

And sent them back to the bar
for more beer, more bragging.

The woman who had been raped yet again
put her head down and cried.

Carrier is proud of what they have done for science, for tourism.
A triumph of technology. A triumph for America.

We know what to do with the body of an adolescent girl
so the public will gawk at her for hundreds of years.

"It wasn't rape," protested one of the five men who carried
Krista's limp body from the bathroom into a dark booth.

"It was a gang bang. She didn't say yes
but she didn't say no."

We don't call it rape
because it is part of our culture.

FROM MY GRANDMOTHER'S LIPS

Neatly, carefully, he wrapped each piece.
An ankle stuffed into burlap. A wrist
bound with brown paper and string.

It was Harlem, 1911. My grandmother,
home with diphtheria, watched through the window
for the parish priest as he took his daily walk,
a package under his arm, his free hand waving
to the little girl he knew from Sunday Mass.

Harlem was safe in those days, my grandmother
told me. We never even locked our door.

Her father was sexton of the parish. He walked the church
at dusk, picking up litter, watering plants. When he dug
graves, he wore bits of earth home under his fingernails.

We don't know the name of the dead woman.
We don't know what colour her hair was, or her lips.
The newspaper article called her a prostitute.

The parish priest killed her. Then he cut her into pieces:
feet, hands, wrists, ankles, chest, hips. Her heart. Her eyes.
He took her to a trash can in the park,
one piece at a time, wrapped up nice and neat.

I picture the scattered body parts — an elbow, a thigh —
buried and decaying. A dandelion, that common
weed, growing from her lips. Milkweed between her ribs.

My grandmother told me this story.
It was Harlem, 1911. Women knew their place.
The Church was always right. And you could trust
the world that walked past your door.

AMBROSIA

I wonder if my fear of death
comes from my childhood image of God
as an old white man
standing in the clouds

I mean, men with absolute power
can be such assholes

WHAT WE LEARN

when you walk alone at night
carry your keys in your fist
points sticking out
past the knuckles
just in case

on the train
stare at the floor
read the ads overhead
don't look into the face of a man
it would be an invitation

when men on scaffolds
whistle and yell
don't look up

this woman I know
talked to a boy at a bus stop
he dragged her to an alley
pulled a knife
and raped her
this is manhattan, said the cop
what did you expect?

act like the world is invisible
and no one will hurt you

krista absalon passed out drunk
unconscious on the floor
in casablanca bar in gouverneur
hey, said the five men
who raped her that night
it was an invitation
and the judge agreed

when you have to act all the time
like the world is invisible
you become so small
you become nothing

Pieces of Desire

BITS OF DESIRE

Waking: your dream self lingers on my tongue.

> Voice: chant into me so that I may
> swallow your words.

Driving: I change radio channels until I hear a bit of you.

> Words: I study the way your hands
> move across a page.

Undressing: I wriggle my jeans off in front of the mirror.

> Dance: I breathe you in.

Eating: I wet my lips with just a bit of juice from the core.

> Touch: when you brush against me
> seeds fall from my skin.

Painting: the brush becomes an extension of the tongue.

> Map: surfaces of you I have not yet explored.

SHINING WET

I like the way it tangles and glistens
in my hair. Dream fluid. Milky words. Unspoken
secrets from your cloudy interior self. Words you never
tell me. Droplets of salt marsh at dusk. Your meteor
showers. Your hidden pools.

I want what is inside you. What percolates beneath the layers.

>   *(I need your drowning)*

Streams of hazy dream words. Silken
condensation of your voice. The beating
of the wings of crow. The burst pods of milkweed.
The broken doorways. Warm white tears.

>   *(I look into this doorway of you*
>   *and I say, something is broken.)*

>   Snow trickling from pines. Melt drops
>   splashing. I hold them gently in my mouth.

>   *(You drown in me)*

Spit them into my hands. Glistening self
words. Rubbed into my palms. Memories melted
and viscous. I feel your fingers touch
the person you need me to be.

>   *(the woman I am not)*

I cannot swallow
          the wet, shining, jagged, silent syllables

          cannot take in
          all that darkness

                    swallow
                    all that starry light

LAPTOP

the screen glows
in his eyes
as he works
fingers teasing
words from keys
she bends
to breathe his scent
hair brushing
breasts touching
teeth sweet
against neck
her tongue licks
his eyes shut
her legs dangle
into his lap
keys bite into her
balanced on the edge
words flow through her
she moves
his hands
from the keys
onto her thighs
I am here
she says
pour your words
into me

THE WATERS OF ROUND LAKE

He undressed her in that wavy
mirror, touched the curve
of her reflection, kissed the rippling

until the woman in the reflection
kissed him back. He took
that mirror woman home

to make love to her
in daydreams. She cried his tears.
He knew how to hurt her.

She wanted to wrap his wounds
with her hair, slip
her tongue into his darkness.

He looked into her eyes
to see himself. He sipped
the milk that dripped

from her breast. She licked the salt
from his skin. Until their souls
stuck together with saliva and sweat.

They didn't know how
to heal each other
without drowning.

One summer night
he shattered the mirror
breaking her into shards.

He knew he could not
touch her again
without bleeding.

ROCK

When his layers buckled
in frozen waves, she melted
them against her breast, breathed
hard against the glacial crust, licked
     the icicles of sweat

When his layers ignited,
     burning, raging,
the taste of his ashes
woke her from dreaming

Stop destroying the layers, he screamed
     Those layers are me
     They are who I am
     There is nothing else

But she kept on gnawing
     with teeth and tongue
     biting, tearing,
until they were both writhing
overwhelmed by   frozen   burning   wetness

She dreamed his dreams
He knew how to hurt her

She gave him her words, her tears, her breath
It wasn't enough

He pressed his weight against her
ground her into fragments

These layers are me
he said

You are nothing

CAGED

She sees herself in the glass.

Clouded leopards pace
in darkness. Birdsong echoes
off concrete sky. Feet tramp slippery planks
above a fox who hides from pointing fingers.
A child screams to be free.

Her wings, bruised and aching, curl tight within her.

Rain drips onto wolves who pace
a muddy dog run, elephants born
to asphalt, bison shedding ragged
clumps of fur. The bald eagle broods
with wings that never touch sky.

She paces in this maze of mirrors.

Bighorn sheep climb an alpine
parking lot. Coyotes curl
into balls on mud. An african lion growls.
Other animals crouch
on muddy islands in silence.

If together they rose

her bear claws, her eagle wings, her lion legs, her coyote snarl,
an unswerving rush
of feather, fur, sheep, leopard, woman
could crack bars, break silence, shatter every pane.
She would open her wings

and taste sky.

STILL LIFE IN PINE WOODS

I guess the coyotes are waiting
for a thaw. The skin of the forest cracked
under my boots as I crept into the lung
of woods to see if she was still
dead. Near her throat, a single leaf
clung to stem, as if expecting breath.
Hair frayed the hole in her chest, a tunnel
into the deepest part of her. She must have
struggled for air as she wove a blood trail
through brush, running until she came to the center
of the woods. The center for me, I mean, near
my favorite fallen tree. How many times
I've climbed this log, trying to balance, pretending
that I am no longer afraid of heights. Snow filled
her outline, white belly protruding beneath crust,
brownish legs stretched against shaken
powder. I am not afraid, here, in the cervix
of the woods. She ran to this thicket, lay her body
near my tree, breathed her last warmth beneath
pines that creak and chime under wind. The coyotes
will come, in the spring, when their hunger
is fierce.

GESTURE

in the kitchen sink
          (desperate to touch)
i plunge my wrist into rushing hot water
          to feel the red rash
flame with itch
          (tingling, urgent)

we hiked through lush poison ivy
                         (it was only once)
glossy leaves brushing ankles
          (that throbbing music)
crushed, juicy, waiting
                    (oh that silk)
neck hairs lifted
     wet by river wind
               (sweet drops of sweat)

we washed arms and legs
at the end of the dock
               (skin rubbed damp)
splashing water over calves
and elbows

a futile gesture
          (lips to palm)

our bodies
would remember

SACRED TEARS

This man sent an email
about a nun in Guatemala
who had been beaten and raped.
Wow, he said to the listserv audience.
I find this disturbing.

I remember the time
he pushed me to the floor,
pressed his weight against me,
and said, "I need you to want me."

I had a dream in which he said
I want to talk to you.

My friend Sofia has a child with leukemia
who sleeps on his left side
because of the IV in his right arm.
My son, she says, my heart, my eyes.

I had a dream in which he said
I am sorry.

The man who was disturbed
by what he reads on the internet
leads a comfortable life.
That girl from the supermarket, he says,
she's an easy fuck. It's convenient.

In communities touched by toxins
clusters of leukemia appear
killing children and babies.

Leukemia can be cured, say the doctors.
Two years of chemotherapy, of vomiting
and headaches and weekends in the hospital,
perhaps a bone marrow transplant,
and he will be fine. Maybe.

The man who sent the email is missing pieces
of his childhood, chunks sliced and stolen
by his drunken father. He has empty places
inside him. He fills them with the sacred tears of women.

We could prevent leukemia, say the scientists.
Eliminate the poisons our children breathe and drink.
It's not practical, say the politicians.
We have to worry about the economy.

The man who sent the email
used to lurk in the corridor
near my desk. Some days
I ran to the women's room to vomit.

I had a dream in which he was crying.

The Mormon preacher in Utah
said breast cancer was God's will.
Maybe so. God didn't stop
the government-paid scientists
from setting off atomic explosions.

Don't worry, the scientists said.
We can fix things. We have a solution.
Let us cut off your breasts.
If each woman sacrifices a breast,
things will be okay. Maybe.

Sofia brings her skinny three-year-old
into a room sacred with visions, where people
say they have seen a woman appear.
She begs the translucent madonna
to save her child. Her heart, her eyes.

The man who sent the email wants to die
but he doesn't know how.
He dreams of women made of glass.
He breaks them into shards,
rolls in the broken bits until he is bleeding.

I had a dream in which he was drowning.

The scientist says, I want to tell you
about leukemia. I want to draw you a map
and tell you where it is safe to raise kids.
But I am paid to just fix things.

The man who sent the email told me once:
I am trying to see how many women I can score with.
I like women with big breasts, he told me.
His email about the nun who had been beaten and raped
was forwarded from another listserv.
He didn't know I would read it.
Or maybe he did. He lives in so many realities
that sometimes he gets them confused.
On Sundays, he hates all nuns.
On Mondays, he tries to screw married women.
On Tuesdays, he fucks the woman from the supermarket.
(It's her day off.)
On Wednesdays, he is a sensitive guy
who gets very disturbed when he reads
about a nun in Guatemala getting raped.

The doctors said
Let us take two years of his childhood
Two years of pain
and we can fix him.
Maybe.

The man who sent the email
says: When in pain, screw
the nearest woman.
Make her cry.

WOVEN FROM DARKNESS

Night at Mount Saviour

My scars open at dusk.
The monks weave robes from darkness.

I would drink his words
until I was drunk with him. I lost
myself in his voice.

The poet says
words will heal me.

The monks give silence as a gift.

Vigils 4:45 a.m.

After prayer comes dawn.

The shadow woman weaves
strands of glimmer
into creek song.

When I look at him
all I see is the way
his wounds are bleeding.

I tug on the poet's sleeve.

Brother Bruno feeds the sheep.

The poet says
to write my body into a poem
write myself into a poem.

Laud 7 a.m.

> I have an elusive, slippery
> self. A self used to being
> invisible.

Sky enters the chapel
falling in patterns
on stone floor.

> The shadow woman carries
> her scars in a canvas bag.

>> The man with the scars liked
>> to hear me cry. He told me this.
>> Whenever he hurt me, it made
>> him feel real.

Mass 9 a.m.

People enter the chapel
through four doors -
east, south, west, north.

> I gave him pieces of myself
> until there was nothing left of me.
> I gave pieces of myself
> and it was never enough.

> The poet melts together
> fragments of dream and memory.

>> The man with the scars says:
>> when in pain, screw
>> the nearest woman.

The monks trail
puffs of incense
and prayer.

The shadow woman
shows me the snake
wound about her neck.

My body is me.
Sometimes that is all a man sees.

Sext 12 noon

In the sheep pastures
that stretch above the Chemung River
you can hear the clanging chapel bell
call the monks to prayers.

Something in me has this need
to heal wounds.

The shadow woman cooks over
a fire, stirring a broth
made of desire.

Brother James walks, limping,
to sweep the guesthouse.

None 3 p.m.

I spent so much time looking for him
that I never found myself.

Candles burn. In the crypt
the 14th century stone woman
holds a child in her arms.

He sliced me thinner and thinner
until finally I pulled the pain
from my body to strike him back.

The poet listens to the child
singing in my womb.

Dark figures kneel before her.

Sometimes I hate myself
for the way I give men
power over me.

The stone walls breathe silence.

The poet shows me how to use words
to find myself. The poet says my self
is worth finding.

I could never resist his scars.
Let me tell you about my dream,
he would say. It's about my
father's suicide.

A single cricket chirps.

Vespers 6:30 p.m.

My problem with men is that I always
forget I'm not their mother.

I am wrapped in chant.

The shadow woman says
listen to your dreams.

The man with the scars
pulled down all the invisible walls
until the room filled with his pain.
There was no room for me.

The monks bow their heads
before the stone woman.

I sweep the spaces of my body.

The poet says the poem will heal me.

I still have pieces of him.
I don't know how to give them back.

Compline 8:15 p.m.

Brother Pierre plays the harp in candlelight.

I dreamed a monk
who came to me in the night
and said only you have the power
to forgive yourself.

Vigils 4:45 a.m.

At Mount Saviour
the monks are praying.

The poet works deep in the earth
digging for words.

The shadow woman sleeps in a tent
touched with moonlight.

The man with the scars appears
in a dream. I know that one of his
new scars is me.

RECIPE FOR POWER

When the corporate men
crowding the dinner party table

start bragging about racks

showing off guns
fishing rods
and other long objects

I like to change the subject

I ask the women in the room
what they think about infant circumcision

Works every time

Je voudrais parler d'amour

GARE SAINT LAZARE

dressed in camouflage
he hurries into the train station
finger on the trigger
of an automatic weapon
the leafy pattern of his pants
outlining his legs against grey
stone arches where a woman
beckons to customers
flashing white ruffles
above long dark legs
that stretch beneath
puffs of smoke
men in uniform
jabber in french
gun barrels catch sun
filtered from high glass ceilings
trains keep coming
releasing schoolchildren
a woman in tight red
he pauses to flirt
flashing white teeth
weapon cradled at his side

LA VEDETTE DU PONT NEUF

bridges pass overhead
rhythm moves through muddy water
        to her lips
        her tongue
shadows touch his shirt
a dance of shimmer on white

red geraniums sway
a man tosses bags of potatoes
        pomme de terre
from pier to barge
burlap bags spin in dusk above
        the dark seine

stone glows soft at the curving
edge of luminous night
trees glisten grey and brown

five boys dance naked on the bank
gyrating for the gliding boat

two men on pont neuf
argue and gesture
groping at darkness

she leans over the rail
leans into his voice

cezanne's bathers
stretch naked
into blue green light

pretend we are lovers
she says

he says
this doesn't feel like pretend

JARDIN DU LUXEMBOURG

Branches flower purple against stone.
Old men gather to play chess
in the dust. A nun hurries with her shopping.

Stone statues soak in sun. Green lawns
curve in crescents trimmed with orange.
Feet scuff dust into bloom.

In *le petit jardin* bright ribbons
and ponytails bob above the black rail.
Mothers drowse in spring sun.

The baby nursing
at his mother's breast
drinks colour and sunlight.

NOTRE DAME

The priest disappears into
a storm cloud of incense.
The organ player has gone mad
hitting frenzied notes that echo
against the vaulted ceiling.

Old women in Sunday dresses
sit in woven chairs connected
by wooden rods.

Herds of Americans follow
a red pompom dancing on a stick.
They point and stare,
take pictures of gargoyles
tamed by daylight.

They do not see the swallows
diving below the stained-glass dome
dark wings tipped with night.

SHOPPING IN MONTMARTRE

I undress in a riff of traffic
and footsteps. A dog pushes
his nose against the curtain
to nuzzle my bare legs
as I wriggle out of jeans.

Dark eyes watch as I step
into a square of sun
trying these tight pants
that silk dress.

A woman in white and black
dances in front of the mirror
hips moving above high heels.
Women call to each other
over racks of creamy linen.
The mime on the street corner
sweeps sunshine into broken bits.

I want to taste the rich colours
of this slanting street—
glowing fruits, bolts of fabric
bright awnings, bold umbrellas.
I wrap my neck
with deep blue and purple.
I touch my body
with brick red silk.

CITY STREETS

They crave cut flowers—orange, yellow, crimson—bursting
from cones of crinkling paper. They long for fragrant
french cigarettes with shining
blue wrappers. They savor
wine that will rub their throats
with ruby.

Separated from earth by concrete and brick
they sew desire into red umbrellas, yellow awnings.
They linger in the patisserie to breathe baking
dough, gaze at windows filled with strawberry tart,
clutch fresh baguettes as they descend deep
into the musky rush of the metro.

Bodies touch, knees against
knees, in the train. Hips move in tight
black pants. Dark eyes rove breasts.

At dusk desire spills
onto narrow sidewalks
dancing to the clink of thick cafe mugs
swirling through onions and garlic
and cigarette smoke
below balconies
lit with flame.

CANDLELIGHT

rosary beads swish
                against wrists
      canvas
            shopping bags thud
       onto stone floor

an old woman rubs prayer
      into her fingers

             in this sanctuary of dark

muffled voices map
      the crypt
                curving stone
          walls hold
              twisting flight
       coins clatter
          into a black metal box

flickering   bowls of wax
      light   curve of wrist

        she
      weaves between
glowing trays
      bending to breathe
         white pools
      of melting

FACES IN THE METRO

our train rattles
through dark tunnels
jerking and halting
doors flung open
with gusts of dank

your nose rubs my cheek
breath against skin
stone arches disappear
tiled walls flash
a maze of secrets

cut flowers burst
from paper cones
football scarves hug
unshaven faces
newspapers crackle
beneath fresh baguettes

lip to eyebrow
tongue to chin
together we travel
deep into the earth

in the next seat
a young magician
practices sleight of hand
the coin moving in and out
of slender fingers
while his dark eyes rove
from hip to breast
from face to face

GIVERNY AT DUSK

Mud against skin
her body swallows colour
as Monet's garden dissolves

to grey and black. Roses tickle
her neck. She sips flower burst.
Her body turns to face

luminous scent. Her pores crave
rouge, jaune, doré, bleu. She hoards
colour on her tongue.

His paintbrush winds wet
through cricket song to lick
hair cascading over stone wall.

She drinks the pink of tulips, the yellow
of lilies, the red silk of roses. Her roots
stretch through mud to absorb rhythm.

He hurries to sketch her body,
paint her breasts, brush onto canvas
changing curves, the disappearing light.

Her limbs tangle him
into the garden, into dark
scent and wind

her body
ready to burst
with brilliant dawn.

PARIS FLOWER SHOP

Beneath rippling yellow
the man chooses for his lover

one blossom at a time. He arranges
each fern, brushes petals to his lips.

Shadows reach across pavement to pots
of red and purple. Heels clatter past.

His hands curve to cradle stems
that drip. His silhouette unfolds

for one final swift movement—
to twirl the bouquet into dusky paper

claiming the damp ferns
pushing colour deep.

BIRD MARKET

The hands of the vendors dance
above the trapped music of tiny birds.

The man selling roses offers a kiss
to each woman who approaches.

A little boy in a green shirt and rollerblades
weaves between empty bottles on Pont Sully.

Trills and chirps spill into sunlight.
Songs stain cage after cage.

In the oval rooms of Musee de l'Orangerie
a woman makes love under water

swimming under brush strokes
beneath water lilies that curve open.

Prisoners sang in the conciergerie.
Sang on the way to the guillotine.

Cracked asphalt holds a gnarled tree
that reaches upward to touch sky.

Les amoureux share a bench splattered with sun
chewing through crust baked with butter.

Cages form pyramids of twittering song.
Cages hang below awnings of bright.

A woman sweeps the sidewalk
her knees sore from Sunday kneeling.

I walk into this canvas
to buy blood red roses.

WINGED VICTORY

Her wings fan scent
against his neck as she wraps him in strong
stone legs, carries him past windows that billow red
behind cast iron curves and narrow alleys lined
with polished wood, across rooftops
that clutch brick chimneys, over courtyards
that capture afternoon sun and a river that purrs
under arched grey, through saxophone music
and cigarette smoke and waves that lick
narrow quays.

She rubs her marble breasts
against his warmth until they melt
into flesh.

Other voices

ANCIENT RHYTHM

Uphill toward outstretched pines
panting, I climb.
The baby burrows
her head under my shirt, sucking
until I stumble—
when she cries, milk dripping, I pull close
her squirming body, her rooting mouth. Rocks scrape
the ankles of my searching. My hair hangs
into her face, a few mossy strands pulled taut
by her fists. Her eyes close, body relaxing
with each warm gulp. Past tattered birch
and dark cliffs, step by step,
my body weaves an ancient
rhythm. I learn to cradle her head against my breast,
my elbow pressing her legs into the hollow
of myself. Time coils
its thickness around my
shoulders as I plod upward, leaving footprints
in pine needles. Looking ahead
and not down, trusting
my feet to the ripening August earth,
I walk with other women
who in other times
have climbed
this hill
babies at their breasts.

SEX EDUCATION

the nuns taught us about our bodies
as if men did not exist

thursday mornings
the boys off at gym class
we gathered inside a square of sun
beads clicking
as the woman we called sister
moved and talked
about growing and bleeding
about flesh curving into breasts

she said nothing about makeup or fashion
high heels, nylons, anti-wrinkle cream
this woman in the dark
cotton dress

it was safe
in that fifth grade classroom
to say

this body is for me

this body is for me

DANCING WITH SUN

his body slithered
to disco music

a hockey player from the rez
with serious eyes
cat-black hair

sunny taught me to dance
  hands brushing my velour shirt
    voice purring into my neck

     pounce on the beat
song swirled
through my hips
     as we moved together
   sneakers squealing
on beer-slopped floor
    lean back

i surrendered to music
  to rhythm and swish

     let your hair fly
around me
  jiggled bodies
sweaty faces
  a blurred crowd

swept clean by my hair
  as it spun away from me

    gold

BEAUTY RITUAL

we'd crowd to smell her neck
oh yeah   that's the one
to the blare of bob marley
we got a party tonight
julie sprayed her perfumes
miro   he's going to go for that
hips swishing   we traded clothes
atierno   you cannot wear that
mumbi's clothes came from paris
silk and linen   soft scented
jeri dressed and undressed me
try this colour   feel this fabric
silk purred against my hair
sending sparks into music

during slow songs
i rubbed oil between rows and rows
of braids on mumbi's scalp
we massaged each other
bodies spread on the bed
jeri flirted with the mirror
moving shoulders to the beat
when the music got fast
mumbi jumped up
dark hips wrapped in white
judi waved shirts   purple satin
yellow silk   even while she danced

lost in the swish and thump
of dance   sometimes
we forgot the party
we'd order pizza   savor
steamy slices   our bodies sprawled
amidst piles of colour
wet towels and silk

RECIPE FOR HEALING

The teenagers from Chicago
yell above the hum of their hormones

yeah, ya whore, ya bitch,
yeah, ya motherfuckers

When they think no one is watching
they run up the sand dune
squealing and pushing each other
trailing clouds of sand

At the bottom
sneakers and boomboxes
lie abandoned
like crutches at Lourdes

SILK CREEK GATHERING

We gather in the woods to watch the creek
weave her song. Mary sits at the edge, writing.

I breathe in the yellow smell of autumn.
Clara spreads food onto a blanket.

We weave our lives together,
unravelling sometimes, looping back.

Water ripples, swishes, tumbles,
spills cool droplets into our daydreams.

In Navajo the parts of a loom are named
after the parts of a woman's body.

Weaving is the body telling its story,
yarns spun from wool and history.

We eat pita bread, hummus, grapes.
I brace myself against a tree.

The creek sings its history.
Women talking, water dancing.

DOING CHI GUNG WITH JUDY

Put your head in the crack in the sky
    the geese made

Why stay on this earth?

Grip earth with your feet, your toes
Go where your shadow takes you

I looked at the faces
around the table
all the broken bits of light

Push the ball of energy
between your palms

I want to wash my hair
with shadow and dream
with luminous words

Close your eyes
and let the current take you

Offer parts of yourself
to other creatures

Roll the energy
from hand to hand

Let them devour you
if they must

Surrender

MARSH IN SUMMER

dusted with golden pollen
she lies waiting
for summer thunderstorms

layers of silk and muck
rich humus held together
with weeds and water lily roots

kids pick brown cattail punks
to poke into campfires
duck hunters scatter beer cans

she wears fragile shining wings
bright jeweled bodies
emerald bottle flies singing

rare water lilies scattered carelessly
where anyone can pick them
purple loosestrife beyond control

a dead turtle floats
bloated amidst the lily pads
carp flick their tails

just before dusk
silver spreads
across her stillness

when I try to stare deep
she gives me back
my own muddy eyes

EVENING VISIT

I step from dusk into corridors of light.
A hothouse scented with lilac, clorox, and urine.
Rosa grabs my hand and speaks rapidly, passionately,
in a language I don't understand. Old women
sit patiently on a flowering couch. Hello, they say, hello, hello.
Their fingers clutch at me, savoring the chill
of outside air, the scent of new snow and night stars.
Hello, hello, hello. Wheels hum along the hall.
Folded linen piled high, white towels, white sheets,
pastel blankets. The plastic smell of a new
catheter bag. Tubes filling with warm yellow.
Linoleum scrubbed clean, bleached to pale bone.
Always this stripping away, this wearing down.
Ed pushes his oxygen tank with him, pauses
to say hello. Lynette shows me a purse stuffed with trinkets—
photographs, books, somebody's teeth. Rosa stares
into my eyes, cries when she sees my dark-eyed
son. Always the smell—the thickness
of memories, the past peeling away. Midge holds
my hand as I walk her back to her room. The aides
wash each body. First this limb, this side, roll
and wash, one body, then the next. Women hunch
over pink trays of food, pull clean floral nightgowns
over scrubbed breasts. Brilliant lights stroke
the wrinkles, the old skin, the blue veins and liver spots.
The body unpeeling, unfolding, stripped away.
Until all that remains is the radiance.

TOBEY HOUSE

She could smell ghosts
layered beneath wallpaper
in the room where she slept
moonlight touching suitcase
left open on wooden floor.
She could hear them
creeping softly from lavender roses
to sip the cup of breastmilk
left on the nightstand.
Little girl ghosts pranced on her bed
leaving finger smudges
as they peered into her dreams.
Tobey cat stepped from her childhood
to nestle against the curve
her hip made with the quilt.
In the huge dark house
miles from her own warm baby
she slept, protected by
a woman ghost in a long skirt
who recognized her full breasts
the worn texture of her hands
who hushed the children ghosts:
Shh. She's tired. Let her sleep.

AFTERNOON REIKI

I understand long limbs because I know oak trees
the way they stand silent at marsh edge
stubborn branches reaching for sky.
Sweeping light across the long path of his body
from sweaty lion hair to bare soles
made me reach beyond myself. I recognized
the writing on his palms, the hands of a healer,
knew what I'd find when I pressed against them,
and yet, when violet light drenched me, I laughed aloud,
my voice vibrating through the shifting butterfly colours of him.

Snakes of yellow and orange slithered across his body
the way sun coils against island rock, tingling beneath
my palms, so hot that when his eyes blinked open,
like someone just waking, I almost fell into the blue.
Perhaps it was the water-coloured t-shirt
he wore, or highway traffic rushing river light
through pulled blinds, or the single beeswax
candle with its cleansing flame. I saw my whole self
in that iris, gathered inside petals pond blue.

WOVEN

                    Roone's voice
leads me into the garden I carry inside of myself.
Past stone walls, cornfields, a cave of red clay. I swallow
seeds to fill myself with sunflower light.
                    Spirit guides ripple
through this circle of women. Flicker of feather
and breath. We thank sky and earth. Butterflies carry pollen
from wrist to wrist. We breathe smoke of sage and sweetgrass.
                    We carry earth
under our fingernails. We grow hemlock and
hostas, simmer fragrance over flame. We wear
essential oils, dishwater suds, poison ivy rash.
                    We stand safe
inside columns of light, touched by translucent cascade
of sparkle. We are woven together in this circle of shining,
elbow to elbow, our feet on the ground, rooted and strong.
                    We ask blessings
from twittering birds, cars humming past, kids playing
in the street, the pine tree who rubs her branches
against porch and window, against sky.
                    We give ourselves
to violet sunset fire. We grow flowers over scars, plant seeds
into soft spots that ache. We leave this earth to return
to this earth to find that we are made of earth. Oil and dirt.
                    We latch
our gates, helping each other lock tight
our dreams, our inner gardens, our blooming.
When you are ready, Roone says,
                    open your eyes.

This is my body

DREAMERS

Legend says
that the Aztec ruler Montezuma
would seek out anyone
who dreamed
about the fall of his empire

He made a list of these
dreamers
and had them killed

Men in power
have always known this:

dreams
are dangerous
powerful

Dreams change things

HER GARDEN

That last day, as she threw clothes and books into the car,
he yelled his intent to mow over her garden.

So Sunday while he was at work, we arrived
in the driveway, a bunch of women armed with shovels.

We dug every hosta, scooping earth to cover roots. We piled plants
into plastic bags. We worked fast to save as many as we could.

I untangled the deep roots of the rosebush she transplanted
as a bride from her grandmother's house in Michigan.

We lifted smooth stones carried home from the bluffs of Lake Ontario
on picnic days before the marriage began to taste bitter.

Fennel, fragile and lush, clung to the fence. Peonies bled petals.
In an empty pot, I found a snakeskin, coiled and glistening.

Sweat blessed our necks, our breasts, our silence.
We pulled plants from the earth, one by one.

The sage. The daphne. The bleeding heart.
The ferns that brushed her scraped knees.

That evening I planted her hostas in the shade
of my garage. Safe, for now.

MAP DRAWN FROM BLOOD

just before dawn
every month
she reaches over my roof
sprinkling aspen leaves
with white
to wash the stains
gathered inside
this body
until each brittle
echo of memory
melts into glistening
dream puddles
painted silver
beneath dark pines

BODY MAP

I get the weird toes
from my grandmother

The scar on my elbow
is from the time I fell
off my bike

The stretch marks on my breasts
are from that summer

between seventh grade and eighth

when my body
grew like magic

GROWTH

I stand naked in the mirror to watch
myself grow. I purr as I stretch my
self big. I wait on cliff edge
in surrender.

She sleeps in my waters, rocked by my movements,
her blood rich from my breathing, her world muffled
in the cocoon of my dreaming.

I've got stretch marks
that turn silver in sunlight.

From inside this chrysalis
legs begin to kick
her heels against my ribs
turn me inside out.

When I bend to pick a dandelion
the bigness shifts and moves.
I fold the baby into myself.

The sun shines through my translucent body.
Through petal of trillium, tinged
with purple. New reed of spring cattail. Thick mist
bending sunshine into rainbow. Ragged
head of dandelion bursting with seed.

When the moon eclipses the sun
the shadows are muted and soft.

BIRTH PLAN

Here is the plan for the birth of my child. I've taken words
from the dreams of 200 women. I'm translating them
for the hospital staff.

1. No blue hospital gown. No sterile drapes.
When I give birth, I want to be naked. I want my body to choose
the colour of its growing.

2. No enema. No antiseptic wash. No shaving of pubic hair.
If I wanted to shave something, I'd shave my head. Like
Jean-Luc Picard. I've always wanted to be captain of a star
ship. When I give birth, I explore uncharted territory, I move and writhe
into new worlds. I want to go where no man has gone before.

In 1872 an English doctor named John Braxton Hicks discovered
pre-labor contractions. This was sort of like Columbus
discovering America. Some people already knew it was there.

3. No drugs. No epidural.
I want to feel the baby moving, her hard head pushing
through layers of me. My bones shifting, my uterus
contracting. I want to feel birth. I want to know fire.

4. No episiotomy. No amniotomy.
I don't want anything that rhymes with lobotomy.
I prefer to stretch slowly, burning in a rim of panting
breaths, around my baby's head.

Pierre Vellay, M.D. wrote that pregnant women must be "trained in the proper way."
His vision: Laboring women "like expert engineers with perfect machines and carefully
presented information [who] control, direct and regulate their bodies."

5. No pitocin drip. No synthetic hormone to stimulate labor.
Let my baby choose his own birthday. My body does not recognize the ticking
of the clock on the wall.

I don't want to control my body. I want to surrender. Let the darkness soak through me, drip down my legs. Let the pulse of that unborn voice throb through me.

I don't want a needle stuck in my hand. If my labor slows, I'll lie in the sun on a fur quilt and let my husband caress my nipples. I prefer to get my hormones the primitive way.

6. No electric fetal monitor.
I don't need a machine to tell me how my baby is doing.
She kicks, she twists, she somersaults inside of me.

*Robert Bradley, M. D. advocated the idea of the husband as the labor coach.
He liked the idea of natural birth but still he thought that somehow
a man had to be in charge.*

7. No bright lights. No noise. No softball cheers.
Don't give me instructions. My body knows what to do.
Birth is not a team sport. I don't want a coach.
I want my husband's presence. His hands to grip.
His arms a sling to lean the baby bulk against. His face a mirror
in which I can watch my baby emerging.

8. No stupid jokes. No cheerful chatter. No television, please.

I want to listen to the moans rising in my throat.
I want to hear the child singing in my womb.

*In the 1950s a French obstetrician named Ferdinand Lamaze began teaching
something he called childbirth without pain. French Catholics were horrified;
the Bible said that it was supposed to be painful. The Pope, who of course
is the first person I consulted when writing this plan, decreed
that he would allow Catholic women to give birth without pain.
This of course was a great relief to Catholic women.*

9. No delivery table.
I am not a plate of spaghetti. Let me give birth on the bed.
A table works fine for conception, but it's way too hard
and far too awkward for birth.

"Male science disregards female experiences because it can never share them."
Grantly Dick-Read said this in 1933. No one listened to him.

I know what I want for my baby.
No nursery. No pacifier. No bottles. No crib. No cheerful,
white-coated, well-scrubbed, briskly-walking, thermometer-wielding nurses,
please.

Let the baby sleep against my skin, nurse from my breast,
wrap her wrinkled blue limbs in the heat of my body.

10. Nothing intrauterine, nothing intravenous.
I prefer to give birth in simple words. Breathe. Push. Touch. Pain. Wet.
Stretch. Burn. Birth. Yes.

For fifty years, doctors have used these terms:
Braxton-Hicks contractions. Bradley birth. Lamaze breathing.
But a woman knows: the mystery is too overwhelming.
We can never name it.

When the baby's head crowns, I want to touch the wrinkled scalp.
I want to cradle the head in my palms while she is still inside of me,
her neck stuck in the warm swollen parts of me. My moans will be the guide
I need to pull her out of myself.

Hot compresses. Yes.
Dim lights, a bathtub of warm water. Yes.
Hands massaging me. Yes.
My husband lying next to me, solid to lean against. Yes.
The smell and feel of a slippery newborn baby
wriggling against my naked skin.
Yes.
Yes.
Yes.

CHRYSALIS

Hungry crying
stirs me out of dreams
into a dawn
of musty canvas, damp
pillows, ribs that ache.
I crawl over the breath
of a sleeping husband, stumble
out of the tent into a thick
morning

to sit on the ledge, legs curled
against the moss, feeding a warm
baby who nestles
his cheek against my breast,
milk dripping
from the sides of his mouth
as he drifts into sleep.

In the marsh that stretches before me, cattails touch
the mist. Jewelweed opens to warmth. And I wonder

what other woman in what other time sat here
like this, her sleeping son cradled
in the crook of her leg,
watching the great blue heron rise
from her nest, weaving herself
into the pattern of dead leaves and new ferns,
eyelids closed, chin raised

touched by the sunrise, drenched
with the morning,

waiting
awakening

GOLD

If you wait for an August evening, when the cattails
are green-gold-yellow, if you stand long enough
on the edge of the big grey rock, your feet tucked
into the moss, if you wait patiently enough, a breeze
will come from the west, a light wind
that will ripple through the marsh, so that every cattail,
one after another, will turn its gold edge toward you,
flicking sunlight across the bay. If you wait
long enough, stand quietly enough, crouched beneath
the huge old oak trees, you can catch a glimpse,
a movement, something golden and ripened,
molecules of colour moving through humid summer dusk,
gathering strength, drifting, flickering,
touching your face, your hands, and finally your lips.

IMPRINT

I remember
the way she would shove her spine
into mine, her heels kicking
against my ribs, her head snug inside
my pelvis.

My daughter has a birthmark
on the small of her back.

A tattoo created
before name
before meaning
before light

imprinted before the midwife
cut the cord.

I used to wash it with a soft cloth
when I bathed her in the kitchen sink,
careful not to bump her squirming
body against the faucets.

I glimpse it now as she does cartwheels
in lowcut teenage jeans and a shirt of mine.

I like to think that as she moves
through her adult life
the mark will remain,
a reminder.

VISION

Women will sweat. Men will dream.
Grandmothers will celebrate their age.
The sky will belong to the stars and the moon.
Wolves will roam the Adirondack Mountains.
Boys will play with dolls.
Football stadiums will be turned into greenhouses.
We will celebrate the mosquito.
Cows will be allowed to nurse their calves.
Children will play without fences.
Families will sing together.
Disney will go under.
Women will feel safe walking alone at night.
We will eat milkweed and dandelions and cattail punks.
We will drive slower, drive less, stop building highways.
We will take the time to watch sunflowers turn their heads.
When we talk about growth, we will think of the rainforest
and not the economy.
We will remember that snowflakes make the world cosy.
We will learn to love water snakes and earthworms and eels.
Children will swim barefoot.
Rivers will be allowed to overflow their banks.
The bald eagle will rule the sky.
We will admire butterflies without touching, without cutting
them apart, without making plans to sell their wings.
Women will feel safe.
We will take down billboards and make them into picnic tables.
We will build bridges instead of walls.
The militia will grow potatoes and rice.
The navy will record the songs of whales.
The airforce will write legends about falling stars.
The army, after studying a colony of ants,
will take over recycling.
The papers on which corporations exist
will catch fire.

During winter storms, families will stay home by the fire
listening to the old people tell legends.
During August heat waves, families will gather near streams
and rivers and lie naked on the banks.
Golf courses will become sanctuaries for deer
and skunk and teenagers.
Vacant city lots will become community gardens.
Men will know what it is like to give birth.
Women with grey hair will grow it long
and teach children how to weave it into braids.
We will plant trees instead of buying air conditioners.
We will gather around the kitchen table
instead of the television.
We will relearn how to tell stories.
Our leaders will write their own speeches.
Women will feel safe.
Our homes will be places of death and birth.
We will listen to birds singing.
Women who reach the age of eighty
will wear headdresses woven of scarlet and purple.
We will play the piano and the harp
and make quilts out the designer clothes we no longer need.
We will celebrate colour.
We will put clusters of poison ivy in vases.
We will break mirrors and use the shards for holiday ornaments.
Anyone who wants to know what she looks like will have to look
for a reflection in the eyes of someone who loves her.
We will make zoos into daycare centers
so children can swing from ropes and play in moats.
Men will love men without fear.
Women will love women without ridicule.
Gunther and Bruce and Meg will grow our food
and deliver it to us in big bins on Thursdays.
We will learn to eat mustard greens and swiss chard.

Children will learn about sex
not from the computer screen
but from their elders
who will teach them that it is sacred.
Women will take all the high heels in the world
and use them as a tools for planting corn.
Men will take all the pantyhose in the world
and use it to stuff rag dolls
for their sons to play with.
Communities will gather to watch sunsets
instead of reality television.
We will no longer have a separate word for nature.
We will no longer have a separate word for mother.
Men will bake bread. Elders will eat first.
Women will give birth at home in dimlit rooms
with partners massaging them and mothers feeding them soup.
Men will cry in front of their friends.
Women will feel safe.
We will celebrate the energy of teenagers.
Communities will dance together,
old people and young people and toddlers.
All drive-through windows will close.
No one will ever eat alone in a car on a highway.
Strangers will share picnic tables and lentil stew.
The old people will teach children
how to make necklaces from dandelions.
Women will have time to breastfeed their babies.
Nuclear power plants will become museums.
Men will have mood swings.
Women will be proud of their stretch marks.
There will be no such thing as climate control.
We will listen to darkness and crickets singing.
We will build rocking chairs.
We will dry our hair in the sun or by the fire.

When an old person is ready to die,
we will bathe her and sing to her
and read her poetry until she stops breathing.
We will worship in the forest
and in the kitchen, with our bodies
and with wildflowers and with each other.